The
LOVE THE
Book

Kathleen Keating

Drawings by Mimi Noland

CompCare® Publishers
2415 Annapolis Lane
Minneapolis, MN 55441

Keating, Kathleen, 1938-
        The love therapy book / Kathleen Keating: drawings by
  Mimi Noland.
p.   cm.
Includes bibliographical references.
ISBN 0-89638-272-9
1. Love.   2. Psychotherapy.   I. Title.
  BF575.L8K373   1992   92-2424
  152.4'1--dc20   CIP

Inquiries, orders, and catalog requests should be addressed to
CompCare Publishers
2415 Annapolis Lane
Minneapolis, Minnesota 55441
Call toll free 800/328-3330
or 612/559-4800

6   5   4   3   2   1
97   96   95   94   93   92

For one human being to love another human being:
that is perhaps the most difficult task
that has been entrusted to us,
the ultimate task,
the final test and proof,
the work for which all other work
is merely preparation.

—*Ranier Maria Rilke*

To my husband, Fred Schloessinger,
for the love that awakens me

To my children, Matt and Ann Keating,
for the love that delights me

To my therapist, Jinks Hoffmann,
for the love that guides me

To my clients, each special one,
for the love that teaches me

To Triform Enterprises, Ltd.,
Camphill Village Ontario,
The Camphill Foundation,
for the love that inspires me

For the skeptical, the cynical, the hopeless—for all who have lost faith in the powers of love...

I have stumbled, pushed, pulled,
and directed my whole life
toward the expansion of my divine humanity,
an inner largeness
that keeps spreading my soul before me
and expanding my spirit around me.
Something closed and cold within
keeps turning me toward the eternal glow of love
until I melt and overflow
in tears and screams and laughter and roars,
and vitality spins around me like a dance.
I can't stop now.
I have taken risks
on purpose because I believe in love
and accidentally because I was naive.
I not only have been burned, I have been consumed
in the fire of hope.
But after the pain I am always resurrected,
to my amazement, again and again
and again.
Each time I dust off the ashes of experience
I am deeper and richer
and closer to the wonder of who I really am,
and, as the family of humankind,
who we really are.

. . . keep the faith

Like a dragon, love is a magical paradox. Sometimes fierce. Sometimes tender. Always mysterious.

Love is magical because we have spacious imaginations that allow us to be inside the reality of others.

Love is a paradox because its healing power is both simple and complicated, easy and difficult. The decision to become open to love can be hard, but the techniques of love therapy are easily mastered.

Anyone can be a love therapist. This little book can help you be more sensitive in the ways that you give and receive love. Making loving and creative choices is as easy as learning a few basic "dragon dance" steps.

Love therapy is an opportunity for mutual growing and healing. It may be shared by colleagues, friends, lovers, family, children, those related through kinship or kindness—or just with someone passing through your heart.

The dragon is our metaphor because it is an ancient symbol for wisdom and transformation—the magical effects of love therapy. Our dragons are playful, to honor the creative spirit that is the essence of love. May these lively little dragons be your guides on your journey to the center of your heart—where love begins.

PRINCIPLES
OF
LOVE THERAPY

Definitions

love n. deep and tender feelings of affection; strong feelings of goodwill and commitment; v. to feel wholehearted affection, compassion, and respect for

therapy n. treatment, esp. for the purpose of healing, preserving health, restoring wholeness; adj. therapeutic, having healing or curative powers

love therapy n. 1. treatment that heals and restores by means of deep affection and compassion 2. the practice or process of healing through love

Love is a dragon
dancing to a double heartbeat
weeping
laughing
singing
breathing fire
stirring the divided
into harmony.

Love is a dragon
dancing to a
double heartbeat.

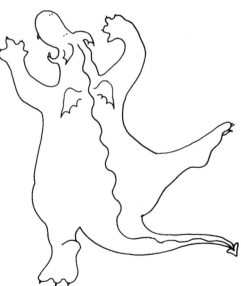

Love is a dragon, dancing to a double heartbeat.

The double heartbeart of empathy means understanding someone's feelings so completely that you seem to be inside that person's heart. Another magical paradox about love is that you can feel another's sadness or joy as if it were your own, but at the same time you feel your own feelings. Two hearts can beat as one, but they are still two separate hearts. The dance of embracing and letting go, of separating and joining again, is honored again and again.

Love is a dragon, weeping.

Love weeps. We are open to the rainbow-range of human feelings, including the pain of loss. As we allow ourselves to feel our needs—and acknowledge our struggle to fulfill them in healthy ways—we are able also to feel tenderness toward others in their struggles. Tears keep us gentle, creating a soft, receptive space within our hearts where we can nurture our dreams and desires.

Love is a dragon, laughing.

Love laughs. We have the marvelous capacity to experience joy, wonder, and curiosity. Because we are blessed by the gifts of humor and play, we keep the faith in love.

5

Love is a dragon, singing.

Love sings. When we listen and speak from a place of empathy, we are exchanging much more than rational thoughts. The dialogue of love has a harmony that restores hope to a wounded spirit.
However,
this love song comes from the head
as well as the heart. To compose
words for love to express its
healing power, we do not
need the mind of a genius
or the morality of a saint.
But we do require some
easily learned
skills.With a little
effort and an open
heart, a love
therapist can
offer messages that
dispel fears,
recover meaning,
and create
alternatives.

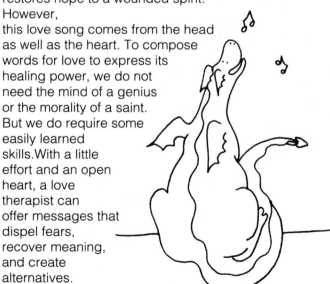

Love is a dragon, breathing fire.

As fire changes matter into energy, love transforms us from creatures who simply exist to courageous beings who live from a deeper purpose. We become universal lovers with an allegiance to cooperation. Our passion as love therapists is to heal alienation, create joy, and live more fully in the presence of earth's splendor.

Love is a dragon, stirring the divided into harmony.

Love is a balancing act, the gracefulness of cooperation in action. Without the constraints of blame and criticism, compassion is free to form and re-form a harmonious whole out of our diverse needs and beliefs. Through the enlivening process of love therapy, we skillfuly explore, collaborate, and negotiate to find a balance of happiness for everyone. The result of love's efforts is a community that celebrates peace.

Love is a balancing act.

Rationale

Love will . . .

open minds
boost spirits
build self-esteem
soften hearts
awaken souls
renew hope
shed light
reveal truth
uncover meanings
add confidence
offer comfort
release laughter
lift enthusiasm
evoke mercy
balance actions
integrate parts
bridge differences

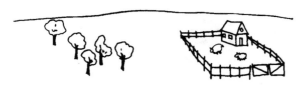

Love carries us aloft.

overcome difficulties
resolve conflicts
bestow power
heal dis-ease
end despair
dissolve walls
untangle troubles
redeem mistakes
create cooperation
harmonize voices
erase hate
discover satisfaction
bring trust
find joy
make peace
unite all
beings

Love therapy is for . . .

. . . anyone who is wounded or woebegone, vulnerable or hardened by the labors of life, trapped, questing, unsettled, edgy, fierce, fearful, recovering from past hurts, dealing with present chaos—or just plain weary.

It is for . . .
presidents, parents, and politicians,
taxpayers, tillers, and teachers,
captives, captors, and captivators,
friends, lovers, passersby,
dreamers and commentators,
leaders and tagalongs,
duos and dynamos,
dancers and counselors,
youngsters and elders
good sports, bad sports,
strays, sellers, and
storytellers,
artists and seekers,
spouses,
ex-spouses,
eccentrics,
explorers . . .
    we are all explorers!.

LOVE THERAPY IS FOR EVERYONE!

Even me?

When we learn to administer love therapy, we also learn to receive it. Love therapy is a circle. Receiving is giving. Giving is receiving. Anyone who believes in the transforming energy of love can be a love therapist.

ANYONE CAN BE A LOVE THERAPIST!

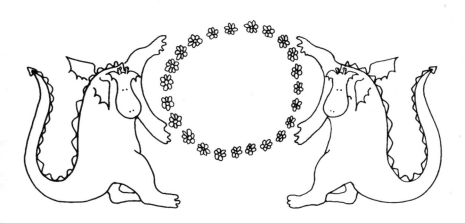

Love is a circle of giving and receiving.

Theory

We have expanded the recognition of our Selves as amazing physical creatures with rich hearts and extravagant imaginations. We now understand that reason alone is not enough to explain the astonishing complexity and paradoxes of the psyche. With new wisdom, skills, and love, we are learning how to mend and weave our feelings, intuition, thoughts, and imaginations into a new wholeness, a new health.

This reach to embrace the whole as well as to respect the parts is our challenge as healers, teachers, guides, and co-creaters of our destiny.

Love seeks to
embrace the whole.

Qualifications

To qualify as love therapists, we apply ourselves with passion to our larger destiny as universal lovers.

Love therapists have a vision of the whole of things. Our desires are congruent with earth's needs. Our total earth community—including all of its inhabitants and the natural world we call our home—is now the primary focus of all efforts toward creating values, purpose, and cooperation based on loving concern.

Love therapists are leaders in awakening to an urgent planetary responsibility. We are called upon to give the world its heart. As we combine our gifts of imagination with our call to serve, we will find that our growing capacity to cooperate, heal, and cultivate beauty will continue to generate the most astonishing transformative power the world has ever known.

Love therapists live by a broad definition of love, which creates a circle of cooperation for all. Intolerance within neighborhoods and nations has unleashed a tragic force of violence capable of destroying our planet. As love therapists, we transform this energy into a vitality that includes all without diminishing the spiritual values of any one society. We respect and delight in our diversity—in the perspective each culture brings to our total humanity. Prejudices dissolve as we heal the wounds of fear.

Love therapists are not captivated by a consumer style of life. Our renewed love for the planet helps us overcome feelings of personal alienation that can lead to paralyzing addictions to material comforts and pleasures. We are no longer untouched by the emptiness in our hearts and the destruction of the environment around us.

Love moves us to preserve the earth...

Love therapists, together, promote the respectful coexistence of all earth's creatures and the guardianship of its resources. Everyone will reap amazing new benefits as our expanded love and alliance enables the life of the whole earth to prosper.

...and all of its inhabitants.

Ethics

Love therapists are willing to be exceptionally responsible for what they say and do. Rules of conduct for love therapists:

1. *Love therapy is ALWAYS nonsexual.*

Love therapy is about using our hearts, minds, and spirits to build bridges of understanding. Romantic or sexual love in an intimate partnership creates a fidelity that supports a special commitment. This personal devotion is different from the universal love that unites all beings. However, physical touching, when clearly nonsexual and mutually agreeable, can be a powerful way to heal emotional wounds. For example, a supportive touch or hug acknowledges the bond of compassion that connects us all.

Love therapists respect
sexual and romantic boundaries.

2. Love therapists are not endlessly indulgent or permissive of all behavior.

A love therapist does not support everything another says or does. Love is not about making a life of continuous ease for others. Enduring to the point of self-sacrifice—allowing oneself to be victimized or exploited—is not love, but a destructive trap for all concerned.

3. Love therapists do not solve problems.

Although we are different in a multitude of ways, we share many atttributes, including a richness of emotions. Because of this commonality, we are able to offer, from our own experience, imaginative options for resolving conflicts or problems. Love therapists are not problem-solvers. Instead, they empower others by offering an abundance of creative alternatives and the freedom to accept, refuse, or experiment with what has been shared. Each person has the exclusive responsibility for making choices and determining consequences.

Recognizing that the process of change is different for everyone, love therapists offer flexible alternatives as a way to stimulate possibilities, without attaching "should," "ought to," or "must" to any of them.

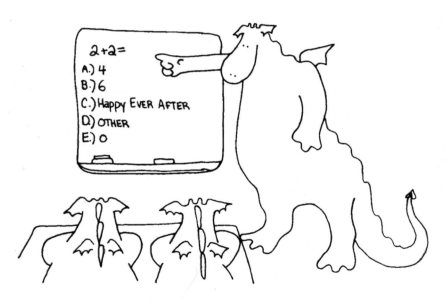

Love therapists offer multiple choices.

4. *Love therapists do not give too little.*

Love therapists know that helping someone heal requires the continuing exercise of empathy and boundless patience. They respect the courage it takes to be candid about an instance of crushed self-esteem, a starved need, or a bruised ego. They respect suffering that is beyond another's capacity to express in words. They empathize with the frightening experience of feeling hurt, lost, empty, helpless, or even weak—especially if those feelings are not recognized as normal. Love therapists are responsive to the timing of each individual in exploring, expressing, and integrating feelings.

5. *Love therapists do not give too much.*

In a healing relationship, the giver holds the position of strength and power. In fact, giving is one of the highest manifestations of power. To give too much or for too long may create dependency and prevent the receiver from returning to a position of confidence and self-reliance. By giving only what is truly needed in a moment of crisis or distress, a love therapist supports another's autonomy and personal power. As love therapists, we are not responsible for finding solutions, gratifying needs, or abolishing pain—only for profound understanding.

Fee

Love therapy is not free. The fee is honesty.

Honesty allows love to circulate freely. This exchange of personal truths is the price paid both by the one who gives and the one who receives. Honesty is the cost required to unmask from our safe, acceptable roles and reveal our deeper selves. Ideal images must fall away to make room for authentic beings to see one another.

When we were very young, we delighted in the wonder of what felt good and gave us pleasure. We accepted and expressed honestly our natural, spontaneous selves. We were responsive and eager to reach out and participate creatively in the life around us. If we were made to feel ashamed of our genuine feelings and needs, we refused existence to those aspects of ourselves that were rejected.

Once we reclaim what was denied us, we can bring caring attention to those places that have been hurt by being cut off from acceptance. Honest love becomes a stream of life-energy that melts through our tough defenses and awakens our basic sense of worth.

Honesty will ransom the lost treasure of the authentic Self.

Side effects

A broken heart is an open heart. When we administer love therapy, we are willing to be vulnerable to pain. Allowing ourselves to feel pain is an act of courage that teaches sensitivity and profound compassion. Suffering is the inspiration for our most humane endeavors.

Often we will be shaken and bruised by feelings that hurt—despair, fear, rage, guilt, shame. Still, they are valuable guides to the parts of ourselves that are most sensitive and in need of healing. When feelings are not explored, pain is trapped within, closing us off from ourselves in subtle ways. When we fully feel and examine the meaning of uncomfortable feelings, without criticism or blame, we find relief, hope, and renewal. The process of moving with insight through the experience of pain is rejuvenating—a letting go and an opening to a new beginning.

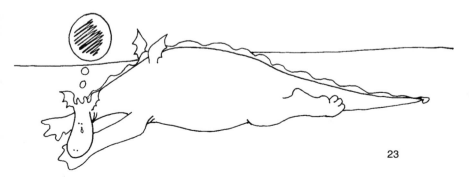

Contraindications

Although love therapy is beneficial to everyone, some may have trouble accepting its true value because they have a limited definition of love. A too-narrow interpretation of love is contraindicated, since it can cause unreasonable expectations, disappointment, and a loss of faith in love's healing power.

Untangle the following love "nots," so the energy of love can flow freely.

I like Mozart.

Love does NOT ask us to like things we don't like.

As individuals, we have distinct tastes, rhythms, desires, and styles of communication. Sometimes these differences bump against each other. At such times, a simple no—or a concise statement of preference—is an act of honesty and love.

I like rap.

Love is NOT just a feeling.

Love is more than a feeling that "just happens"
spontaneously. Love generously respects all feelings—
excitement, fear, joy, sadness, yearning—all the
emotions that arise naturally as we are pulled toward
what we need and pushed away from what causes pain.
But love does not endorse every impulse to act that
might result from our complex feelings. Instead, love is
the work of making responsible choices of words and
actions that support the greater good and happiness of
everyone involved.

Love is NOT limited.

Love is not limited to the drama of passionate lovers, the
devotion of celebrated saints, or the bond that holds
families together. It is a continuous source of power that
illuminates our everyday experiences, an energy that
transforms fear, confusion, and despair into
understanding, harmony, and faith. Love is the radiant
flow of honest words, negotiated decisions, gentle
touches, fluid alternatives, cooperative work, home-made
inspiration, and creativity without end. We discover that
love is all around us and through us as we learn to
access the wisdom and kindness in our own hearts.

Love is NOT passive.

Love is passion. At times, love is called to be the transmuting flame of anger. Anger, created out of love, can be a small signal that a desire is being thwarted or a serious sign of a greater injustice. Anger is the feeling force that motivates action to protect needs, prevent harm, and promote equality. However, the skills we learned in childhood to contain and direct anger frequently are too limited to be useful in our complicated adult relationships. This lack of inner competence can cause feelings of frustration and powerlessness, which may distort healthy anger into blame and destructive behavior.

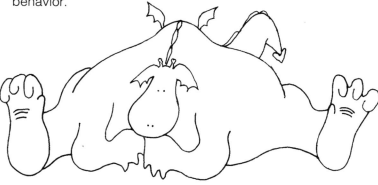

Love is never passive.

Love therapists continually learn and promote methods of managing anger and transforming it into respectful self-assertion. When anger is an expression of love, it is never vengeful or violent, but a passion for justice that benefits everyone.

Anger can be an expression of love.

Lovesickness/ Lovewellness

How we treat "falling in love" is important. In fact, falling in love can be a dis-ease. A hasty or careless approach may cause a painful lovesickness that prevents the development of an enduring love. Actually, "falling in love"—catapaulting head-over-heels into love—is not what happens. In reality, we are "opening to love."

As we grow up, we build walls around our hearts to protect our true feelings and needs from the pain of rejection. These walls are made of controlled feelings, cautious thoughts, dulled senses, stiff movements, veiled glances, and polished behaviors.

Then you meet someone "special," and suddenly, mysteriously, the wall protecting your tender heart begins to tumble down. An opening has been made, and you enter or "fall into" the presence of love. Because the opening into your inner world of love seems to be activated magically by one individual, you attribute the source of love only to that person.

However, what is "special" has to do with this individual's ability to see through your protective wall to the real you. The glory of your divine humanity is reflected in the eyes of the other. What you are falling in love with is the experience of seeing your deepest self mirrored in another. You give credit to the mirror—the other—for the beauty you see reflected there.

But when you attribute your experience of love only to the presence of another, you fail to recognize your own loveableness. If you are dependent on someone else for your sense of worth, you will never discover that your value cannot be measured through another's perception.

When you understand that the love you see reflected in the mirror of another's acceptance is simply a recognition of who you really are, you can begin to accept the truth: YOU ARE LOVEABLE.

In loving, you also become a mirror for the other's genuine self. Whenever you listen compassionately to the other's deepest feelings and needs, you are acknowledging her or his loveableness. The one you love, feeling loved and loveable, in turn experiences you as loving. Together, you create a circle of love.

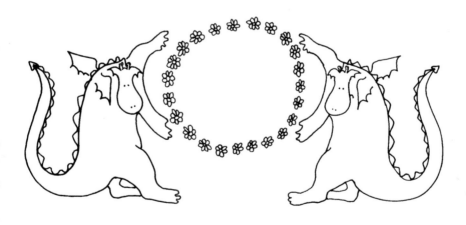

Together, we create a circle of love.

Falling in love, or opening to love, is simply a temporary state of grace confirming the bliss of unity and harmony that is the essential nature of the universe. Opening to love may be the beginning of a committed partnership, or it may be a momentary illumination of what is possible when two meet with open hearts.

We are mirrors for each other.

KINDS
OF LOVE

Love therapists recognize that there are three primary types of love: "Everywhere Love," "Nearest Love," and "Love Within."

EVERYWHERE LOVE is in everyone and everything, everywhere, forever.

This is the ecstasy of union with all beings, when we transcend the confines of culture, race, beliefs, gender, even species. It is the bliss of belonging we experience when all that is particular and exclusive about us dissolves. When differences disappear, all that is left within us and around us is the luminous energy of pure love—a dazzling, resplendent love that is unconditional and boundless.

Love is the stuff we are made of.

NEAREST LOVE is personal, individual, and in space and time. This is what we, each in our own way, create out of Everywhere Love. The conditions of our lives, the borders of our personalities, and the power of our imaginations will determine how we define and embody Nearest Love. This kind of personal love is shaped by the choices we make as individuals in response to our feelings, needs, ideas, wishes, and visions.

We are the stuff we make out of love.

LOVE WITHIN is respect for ourselves as worthy and wondrous beings.

We love ourselves because we are a form of love, unique and delightful embodiments of Everywhere Love. As starpoints of light in the universe of Everywhere Love, we shine with love and from love.

We love the stuff we are made of.

Everywhere Love

Love is not just an abstract idea invented by the human mind. Love is an endless pattern of energy that connects and animates. Imagine a force of light, as blinding-bright as a flash of lightning, expanding into a vast, intricate web—a web of love-energy flowing continuously and forever through every being and every thing. The intense beams of this fine weave of radiance pulse through every creature, every thought, every plant, rock, and river. Everything we know and experience, everything unknown or mysterious, is part of this infinite and pure energy we call love. Love is inside us. We are inside love.

Love is everywhere.

This luminous energy links you to me, and me to you. It is impossible to be alone. Even though we develop as complex, sophisticated individuals with special talents and needs, we are still, in essence, patterns of love that connect.

Love is everywhere.

Because we are joined forever in a current of love, we belong together. We are not meaningless objects existing randomly in space. We fit together as part of the exquisite design of the universe, and therefore we cannot be separated from the home we create with each other and the earth. Alienation is an illusion created by fear. Relatedness is not a choice. Our only choice is in how we will be related.

Love is everywhere.

The unifying power of love provides beauty, grace, and coherence to all of our existence. Every beam of mercy added to the light-web of love alters the pattern of hope for everyone. When we open ourselves to the wisdom that perpetuates this brilliant process, we recover an inner trust and confidence that resonates with the remarkable harmony of the universe.

Love is everywhere.

As love therapists, we embrace and cherish our vision for the whole earth and its inhabitants. We are co-creating a time of rebuilding, when the integrity of all beings and the value of all of nature will guide our activities. Together, we are part of the larger intention of love that transforms the personal meanings of our lives into something shared, something grander than we, as individuals, could ever imagine.

Love is everywhere—leading us to visions and answers, compassion and cooperation.

Nearest Love

Nearest Love, or personal love, is the form Everywhere
Love takes when it is shaped by our resourceful
personalities and the conditions of our lives.

Although we are joined in our deepest awareness by
Everywhere Love, each of us is in a separate body, living
in a certain time and culture, guided by particular beliefs.
All of us have unique characteristics that make us
exceptional individuals. As love therapists, we delight in
the differences that make us precious, unrepeatable
beings.

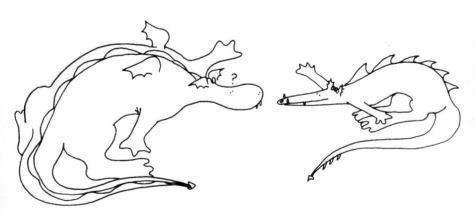

We delight in our differences.

The surprise of love begins in childhood. We are fascinated and delighted by the life around us. Love is everywhere. Yet, even as children, we realize that we have particular likes and dislikes that make up our separate personalities. Nearest Love unfolds as we pursue our individual desires and interests.

We are attracted to certain others because of the satisfaction we feel when we are with them—how fully they correspond with our needs, values, and personal style. Nearest Love emerges when we begin to consider what we want from others and what we are prepared to give. Relationships, like communities, are based on a complex balance of mutual needs and interests, on exchanges and satisfactions.

The intuitive attraction to what and who feels satisfying to us—to what and who makes us happy—is our response to our basic need for Nearest Love. The personal happiness we strive for is not selfish when it evolves from the deeper call of love. When we answer the summons of this kind of love, we make our own, personal contribution to the joy of living.

Nearest Love pulls us toward learning, toward developing our special talents and creativity. It also draws us together in friendship and intimacy to establish relationships and families. By moving toward what we care about and whom we love, we help build "community"—and "community" binds our earth together.

Love and choices

Although falling in love is a powerful feeling state, the value of personal love cannot be measured by feelings alone. It is based on the choices we make to act on our loving feelings.

When we decide to have a relationship with another—as lover, spouse, friend, or colleague—we are doing something specific about the fact that we are all beings united by love. However, a feeling of love is not sufficient reason to build a relationship. When our personalities, interests, values, and goals blend, our mutual desires generate a commitment to share certain common activities of life. Of course, we will always experience conflicts in our personal relationships. But if we use the skills of love therapy, these can be negotiated. Relationships depend on choices, as well as responsibilities toward ourselves and others.

I choose you because...   I choose you because...

Love is not a rarity

Once we discover that love is not unusual or scarce, we are no longer overwhelmed by the experience of falling in love or threatened by what we perceive as the absence of love. For the absence of love is an illusion. We are love. Love is everywhere. Love is the normal condition. Alienation is the exception.

Love is abundant. A love therapist understands that the challenge is to respond respectfully and responsibly to the reality of love's abundance, rather than suffering from the illusion of love's scarcity.

Love is not scarce.

Love Within

We are part of Everywhere Love, and we see our true selves reflected in our Nearest Love. However, we will not experience the true depth of love if we do not have a healthy center of Love Within. This is the self-love at the core of each of us that carries these affirming convictions: "I am worthwhile. I have unique talents." And, most important of all, "I am lovable and capable of loving."

I am worthy and lovable.
(I also dance rather well.)

The ability to love yourself may have been shut down in childhood. Your attempts to find love within your own family may have been discouraged or rebuffed. Or your family may have been supportive, but your school or neighborhood companions did not accept you, leaving you lonely. Because your Love Within has never developed and your concept of Nearest Love has been distorted, you may have turned to a substance or way of life that became first an escape and then an addiction. This crippled you emotionally. Through the practice of love therapy—both receiving and giving—we learn to love ourselves. Renewed self-love creates healing and wholeness.

Love Within—healthy self-love—is not self-centered, but the perspective to see our part in the larger pattern of love. Self-love leads us to respect our own uniqueness, as it allows us to see how we are alike in wonderful ways.

A circle of love

The three types of love—Everywhere Love, Nearest Love, and Love Within—make up a circle that flows both ways. Each kind of love leads to another—and then to another—then back again to the way we first experienced love. Each kind of love demonstrates the possibilities of another kind of love. We need to recognize and express all three types of love if we are to experience the joy of total loving. We need to practice all three if we are to become effective love therapists.

From Love Within. . .
As newborns, we are born with self-love. We know instinctively what we need to survive as physical, emotional beings. And we know that we are important enough to ask for it in irresistibly demanding ways.

to Nearest Love . . .
We bond with others who can fulfill our needs, and out of this bonding we begin to shape our own kind of personal love.

to Everywhere Love.
We translate the lessons learned from Nearest Love to love's broader application: Everywhere Love. And we become universal lovers with a mission of cooperation and peace.

The kinds of love flow in the other direction too.

From Everywhere Love . . .
As part of the love-energy pattern of Everywhere Love, we are also born with curiosity about our earth and universe. (Watch a little one take a walk in a field or a park or down a street, and observe the passionate interest in everything from a caterpillar to a pebble.)

to Nearest Love. . .
We begin to add conditions to our awareness of Everywhere Love—and we ask questions and make choices: How do I want to pursue my personal goals? What will be my closest relationships? Who will be my mate? Who will be my friends? From the answers to these questions, we form Nearest Love.

to Love Within.
Our self-esteem builds as we realize not only the personal satisfactions of our everyday, Nearest Love but our broader contributions as part of Everywhere Love. As we grow in confidence and trust, our self-love is stronger and less easily toppled.

The kinds of love make a circle—each lighting the way to another, each teaching about another. We need all three kinds to be whole.

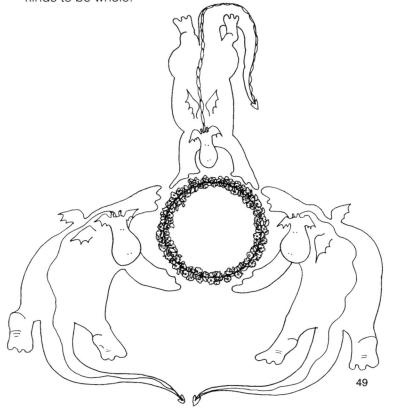

More love "nots"

When Love Within puts blinders on and fails to take up the challenges of Nearest Love and Everywhere Love, it can turn into self-indulgence.

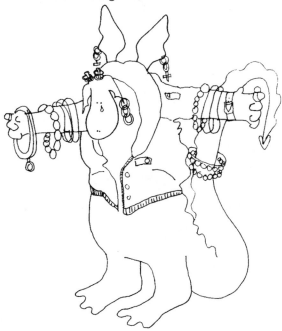

Self-esteem, yes. Self-indulgence, no.

When we open to Everywhere Love and and follow a single, passionate cause, while ignoring Love Within and and Nearest Love, we deny our needs for self-nurturing and intimacy.

Everywhere love should not preempt our personal needs.

When we allow our Love Within to be overwhelmed by the demands of Nearest Love, when we rely totally on someone else—or on the relationship itself—for our self-esteem, it is not love, but unhealthy dependency.

Dependency can be a burden.

THE PRACTICE
OF LOVE THERAPY

Lessons in love

Lesson Number One
Empathy: Discover another's reality

The essence of all love therapy is empathy. Empathy, learned in the dialogue of feelings between individuals, translates the authentic messages of the heart.

Empathy is our ability to imagine, feel, and accept the experience and feelings of others.

We use *imagination*, our brilliant capacity to visualize realities different from our own, to see into the inner worlds of others.

Our *feelings* allow us to participate in another's experience as an equal. Feeling "at one" with another is an extraordinary awareness. From this revelation of "oneness," love develops.

Our *nonjudgmental acceptance* of exactly who others are and what they feel will restore their lost self-esteem and allow for calm, thoughtful reflection about future possibilities.

It requires a "beginner's mind" to enter into the world of another. To do so, set aside your personal judgments, opinions, and advice. Open your mind. Open your heart. Imagine that you are the other, looking out at the world through a different pair of eyes. Let critical thoughts rest as you picture yourself—with as much detail as possible—in the other's circumstances, experiencing the struggle and the anxiety, feeling the feelings. While you are imagining yourself in the other's body, recall as much as you know about the person's life story. With this kind of empathy, you will hold the other's reality almost as if it were your own. Magically, you will discover the appropriate words to express your genuine love and understanding.

For both of you, this honest meeting of spirit with spirit dignifies the struggle and reaffirms your humanity.

Lesson Number Two
Empathy: Discover your own reality

Empathy also teaches us how to become our own love therapists. Through listening with sensitivity, we learn fascinating information about the complexity of our inner Selves. Our curiosity about the intimate reality of others opens us to a new awareness of our own internal world.

Empathy is a lesson in paradox. You learn how to be merged with another and, at the same time, remain a separate individual. Being at one with another requires that you have a separate identity. In the process of supporting another, you maintain self-awareness, knowing that you will not abandon yourself. If you are not centered in a concern for your own rights, you may move from *feeling with* to *doing for* the other and neglect your own needs.

You cannot give others more love than you are able to give yourself. Give yourself the same quality of understanding you give others. Deepen your ability to witness the struggles of your own life with kindness and wisdom.

Every place you reject in yourself, you will reject in others.

When you lack understanding about yourself, you will remain ignorant about others.

When you judge yourself harshly, you will be critical of others.

When you feel shame, you will blame others.

When you fail to forgive yourself, you will be unforgiving of others.

When you lose faith in yourself, you will give up on others.

Your ability to give to others mirrors your ability to give to yourself.

The circle of love must include you. When it does not, the break must be mended.

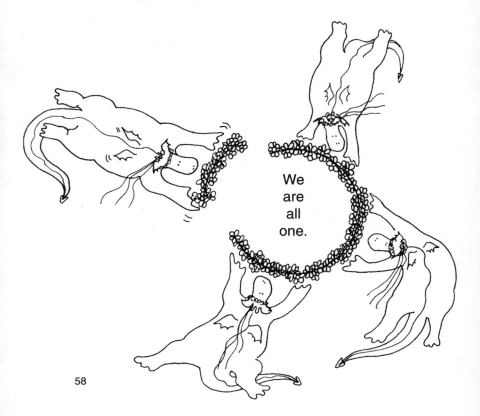

We
are
all
one.

Lesson Number Three:
The dragon dance

For love to become a healing dance, we must teach the head and the heart to move together. Each of us takes a turn leading and following as we practice these simple steps of dragon wisdom.

Following: Take a step back—and listen

Listen with love and understanding, by taking a step back, following the other's words, body language, tone of voice, and feelings. Focus on the other's search for meaning by occasionally repeating in your own words what you hear the other saying and feeling. You do this with empathy by sensing the place within you that knows the same feeling.

From time to time, you will stumble with misunderstanding. But just step back again and give the other room to move forward and rebalance thoughts with another choice of words. You reflect the other's inner wisdom in this exploration of experience. Forward and back, back and forward, the dance of discovering the Self with love continues.

Step back. One, two. . .

Leading: Take a step forward—and speak

When it is your turn to speak, take a step forward and tell the truth about yourself. Begin with "I feel (angry or sad or hurt or happy)." Then describe carefully the situation you are having feelings about. Learn to be discriminating about—and to express—your preferences and needs, instead of judging, criticizing, or blaming yourself or others. Learn the difference between valuing your own ideas and visions and reacting critically to others' beliefs and dreams. To discriminate for yourself, rather than blame others, means to discover what, in all the abundance around you, works or doesn't work to make your life satisfying.

Blaming, by making others BAD or WRONG, imposes your beliefs on their choices and shifts the focus away from your experiences and feelings. When you notice that you are judging, criticizing, or blaming, gently bring the focus back to yourself and what you feel and need.

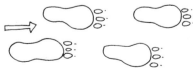

Step forward. Three, four . . .

Moving as one: Do the circle dance—and negotiate

Sometimes, when we can't decide which direction to move in, simply taking turns satisfies both. At other times, when our needs seem to be fiercely opposite, we depend on more advanced love-skills: negotiation and collaboration. After listening to each other carefully and compassionately, we then use our imaginations and creative abilities to negotiate a solution that honors the basic rights and desires of both. For love connects us as equals, as it respects the integrity of our differences. Love integrates everyone's needs in a complementary way.

When the power of love moves in a circle, it redirects the destructive force of aggression and violence onto a path of healing and cooperation.

And . . . make a circle. Round and round.

Keep on dancing: Practice the dragon dance

The goal of love therapy is not perfection. We can't always listen "correctly" or always "say it right." The commitment is to the practice of learning and growing with love. Living is an ongoing experiment in love and truth. What worked today may need to be revised tomorrow. We may feel a bit uncoordinated—even clumsy—at first as we learn the dragon dance, the process that leads to cooperation and mutual support. But practice will transform you into an enthusiastic and graceful love therapist!

Keep dancing, Fred.

Make love

Practice Nearest Love

The myth that we are superior when we believe we don't need others distorts the true nature of independence. When we separate ourselves from our need of others, we become disconnected, lonely, and without love.

When we are *interdependent*, we experience being *connected to* and *belonging with.* We create this sense of belonging and connection by giving and receiving what we need from each other. When we are given to, we feel valued and cherished. When we give to others, we feel capable and worthy.

When I give to you, and you give to me, we ignite a circle of generosity that powers love in action. This flow of energy builds, and soon we are experiencing *making love.*

You are
my special one.

Allow these suggestions to inspire you to create your own acts of love in your practice as a love therapist:

Think of what you appreciate about a friend or family member. *(Thank you for being such a good listener* or *I'm grateful for the wonderful hours you spend with the children* or *I really love your wild sense of humor.)* Write each message on a piece of colored paper, fold it, and put it in a clear glass jar. Label it LOVE TREATS—for use when someone is feeling low in self-confidence.

Set aside the first day of spring as Reconciliation or Remembrance Day. Write or call someone who has been far from your heart or far away in miles. Bring that person back into your life and love.

Buy a theme calendar for anyone who is special in your life—reflecting that person's favorite interest. Personalize it by designating certain days just for the recipient: Hug Day for _____, Appreciation Day for _____. Remember one or two of these newly proclaimed holidays and follow up the calendar with cards or phone calls on those days.

Turn any mis-take into a re-take for someone you have hurt or offended. Give a small, symbolic gift that reflects your remorse. Include a brief letter expressing your regret and what you have learned, making amends, asking forgiveness. (This is also a gift of respect to yourself.)

For a shy child or a reticent friend, make a homemade book of TICKETS TO TALK—each stating "You talk, I listen," each good for one hour of "kind listening provided without advice, available by appointment."

Make a love banner for someone who is ill or who lives far away. Decorate it with personal messages of humor and affection.

Be a love detective. Choose someone you would like to know better and be more caring toward. Ask questions. Notice which situations bring pleasure, which memories are important. Make a list of the person's favorite things, likes, and dislikes. From time to time give or do something on the list. Deepen your understanding and friendship. Watch your love grow.

Personalize impersonal technology with loving acts. If it seems appropriate, FAX a note to your mate. Leave a message of concern or appreciation on a friend's answering machine.

Allow a child to make her own mistakes and learn her own ways of coping. If you rescue her, the lessons are seldom taken to heart.

Allow a child to feel sadness, without trying to "fix" his feelings or erase them. Just, gently, acknowledge them.

Share an artistic wonder. Read together from a favorite book. Listen to music. Explore an artist's work or a philosopher's ideas.

Share a natural wonder—a beach, a view from a hilltop, sight of the sun setting between two buildings.

I'd like to share the sky with you.

Take a bouquet of balloons to someone who is celebrating a birthday—or other special day—alone.

When the moment is right, be a clown for a close friend or two. Make time for laughter—be part of laughter.

Laughter shared is an act of love.

Make Love

Practice Love Within

Learn to be loving toward others by being kind to yourself.

Now and then, plan a day of love and peace for yourself. Seek out your kind of quiet, calming place—an arboretum, a museum, a garden, a park, a shoreline or river bank.

Of course, dragons can fly.

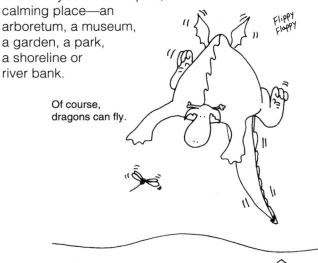

Flippy Floppy

Love yourself enough to entertain all possibilities.

Keep a grumble file. Whenever you feel upset with someone, write a letter stating how you feel (angry, hurt, frustrated) about the exact incident or situation that produced your unhappy feelings, and what you now want. Do not blame. Express only your own feelings and needs. Place the letter in your grumble file until you are able to discuss your feelings in person. When the problem has been discussed, tear up the letter. This is a gift to you in self-understanding and self-worth. (This is also an act of love for the one you care about enough to confront with your genuine feelings and needs.)

Respect your time—choose how to spend it. Each week, mark off private and play time on your calendar.

Next time you pass a park, give yourself a ride on a swing. Let your toes and imagination touch the sky.

Listen to yourself. Meditate to your favorite soft music. Observe your thoughts, feelings, and dreams with compassionate curiosity as they drift by.

Keep a journal. Create conversations between different aspects of yourself. Let your sad or angry inner child talk to the part of you that is wise and nurturing.

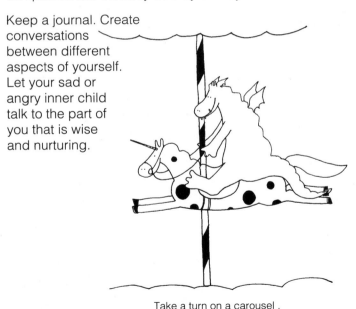

Take a turn on a carousel .

Find a way to express yourself creatively, without comparing yourself with experts. Experiment with painting, poetry, weaving, or other arts until you find something that speaks from your soul.

Put on your favorite music—fast or slow—and let your body move spontaneously. Delight in the movement. Delight in your body.

Dance.
Or imagine yourself dancing.

Buy yourself a big, soft bear—or another huggable character—that makes you smile. Tell it your troubles and hug it often. For all ages.

At least once a week, think of something you appreciate about yourself. Write it on a card and tape it to your mirror.

Every day, affirm your value for simply being you—lovable, loving, and loved.

Make Love

Practice Everywhere Love

Love is power *with,* not power *over.* Love advances only with cooperation and negotiation. This kind of radical love is necessary for our survival. Choose to be involved in ways that allow you to express your unique and creative abilities. Find your own inspiration, and work with enthusiasm, which is the energy of love.

Some everyday acts of everywhere love:

Write a letter to the editor of your local newspaper expressing gratitude for some particular service organization or individual in your community.

Hang up an easily visible chalk or erasable board. Label it "Things to Do Today for Love." Write on it messages of appreciation for earth's blessings, prayers for peace, new ideas for recycling, inspiring quotes, or reminders to contribute food to the homeless.

Buy products that are tested humanely and are environmentally safe.

Have a Recognition Day for store clerks, food servers, bus drivers, bank tellers—people who make your life easier through frequent but essential services. Take time to smile and say thank-you. Celebrate this day until it becomes a love-habit.

Join a group actively dedicated to preserving the planet—to protecting the atmosphere, the forests, our fellow creatures. Appreciate the diversity of life, and the healing secrets waiting to be discovered in this diversity.

Carry a cloth or string grocery bag. Save paper. Save trees.

Honor others' expressions of love and striving for goodness—however different they may be from your own. Respect the beliefs and ceremonies they have found to answer their spiritual needs.

Hold a fundraiser for the earth. Invite a group of friends for an old-fashioned box-lunch auction. (Each contributes a vegetarian lunch in a recyclable or reusable container.) Donate proceeds to your favorite save-the-environment organization.

Listen to native peoples. Study their teachings about cooperation with the earth. Support the preservation of their language and traditions.

Learn which resources, plants, and animals are endangered or threatened

Swim with dolphins (but only in oceans or open bays).

Make choices based on the principles of love therapy.
(Remember the dragon dance: listen, speak, negotiate,
practice cooperation.)

Caring acts do not depend on how much we do, but on how much love flows into what we do.

Be love. Do love. As we practice the art of giving and receiving love, we will continue our whole lives long to deepen our capacity to love. Love is the way our lives began. And this is our destiny—to love, be loved, and add love to the world we live in.

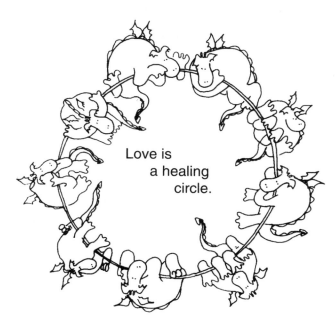

Love is
a healing
circle.

Maybe all the dragons of our imagination
are really our powers of healing.

Maybe they are only waiting
for our courage to choose love.

Love is mysterious . . .

. . . and magical.

Love transforms.

Love yourself.
Love each other.
Love the earth.

About the author

Kathleen Keating Schloessinger, R.N., M.A., is author of the beloved international best sellers, *The Hug Therapy Book* and *Hug Therapy 2*. As a mental health counselor and educator, she conducts seminars and workshops worldwide on "The Nature of Love and Intimacy," "The Power of Touch," "Translating the Heart; Creative Self-Analysis," and "The Wounded Healer." She and her husband, Fred Schloessinger, a psychotherapist, live, love, and work together in Ontario, Canada.

She writes: "Because the grief in my father's eyes and the terror in my mother's heart became my burden of sorrow, and because I live in a world in which the sharp edges of broken hearts become knives of rage, despair, and violence, my life always will be a journey to free myself and others from fear, pain, and hopelessness. By the grace of love, I have learned to keep my passion stirred and my yearning soul alive. I have come to rest in the wisdom that living is about breaking and mending. Since I am forever a part of both, I have chosen the path of a healer, a poet, and a mender of broken hearts—a universal lover.

"I invite you to join me. There is no other way the world can survive."

About the illustrator

Mimi Noland, creator of the renowned bears who demonstrate principles of healthy hugging in *The Hug Therapy Book*, *Hug Therapy 2, and The Hug Therapy Book of Birthdays* and *Anniversaries*, is an artist, writer, and singer/songwriter. She owns and operates a horse farm west of Minneapolis, breeding and training ponies and miniatures. She has a B.A. in psychology, and is certified as a police officer. *I Never Saw the Sun Rise*, her journal of recovery written at the age of fifteen under the name of Joan Donlan, is a best-selling book for young people. *The Love Therapy Book* is the seventh book she has illustrated for CompCare Publishers.

To write to the author

Write to Kathleen Keating at CompCare Publishers. Please send her your love stories and love miracles, telling about love in action through service, relationships, politics, or any other ways, for possible inclusion in her next book. Although we cannot guarantee that every letter will be answered, all will be read by the author with respect and gratitude. Both author and publisher value and learn from your responses.

CompCare Publishers
2415 Annapolis Lane, Minneapolis, MN 55441.
Toll free 1-800-328-3330 or 612/559-4800.

Everywhere love in action

Love means *power with* and not *power over*. Love advances only with cooperation and negotiation. We choose to be involved in ways that allow us to express our unique and creative abilities. When we do what truly inspires us, we work with enthusiasm, which is the energy of love.

The following groups represent just a few of the creative ways people "make love":

Camphill Foundation, Pughtown Road, P.O. Box 290, Kimberton, PA 19442. Over fifty small villages throughout the world dedicated to cooperative living with the developmentally disabled. Triform Enterprises in Hudson, New York, (my daughter Ann's home) and Camphill Village Ontario in Argus, Ontario, Canada, are two villages I support.

Christic Institute, 1324 North Capitol Street NW., Washington , DC 20002. An interfaith, nonprofit center concerned with human rights, social justice, and personal freedom.

The Listening Project, 1898 Hannah Branch Road, Burnsville, NC 28714. An empowerment process that trains activists in listening and better communication. Provides training sessions and a manual.

National Association for Mediation in Education (NAME), 425 Amity Street, Amherst, MA 01002. A source of information about conflict resolution in schools. Maintains a directory of active programs.

The Seva Foundation, Dept. C, 108 Spring Lake Drive, Chelesa, MI 48118-9701. An international development organization concerned with blindness in Nepal and grass-roots empowerment in Guatemala. Sponsors retreats and conferences encouraging compassion in action.

Oxfam, 115 Broadway, Boston, MA 02116. Funds self-help development and disaster relief in poor countries. Sponsors annual Fast for a World Harvest.

Mothers and Others for a Liveable Planet, Natural Resources Defense Council, 40 W. Twentieth Street, New York, NY 10011. A source of information on how families can work for solutions to environmental problems. Publishes quarterly newsletter, *tic*.

Greenpeace, 1436 U Street NW., Washington, DC 20009. An action group that attends to a wide range of environmental concerns, from whales and clean air to toxic waste.

New Dimensions Foundation, P.O. Box 410510, San Francisco, CA 94141-0510. Nonprofit radio sharing compassionate visions for relationships and the world. Audio cassettes available. Supports an ongoing fund for the distribution of programs to prisoners.

The Giraffe Project, P.O. Box 759, 197 Second Street, Langley, WA 98260. Phone: 206/221-7989. Recognizing individuals who risk for what they believe in.

Suggested Reading

Achterberg, Jeanne. *Imagery in Healing: Shamanism in Modern Medicine.* Boston: New Science Library, Shambahala, 1985.

Andrews, Frank. *The Art and Practice of Loving.* Los Angeles: Jeremy P. Tarcher, 1991.

Borysenko, Joan. *Guilt Is the Teacher, Love Is the Lesson.* New York: Warner Books, 1990.

Dass, Ram, and Mirabai Bush. *Compassion in Action: Setting Out on the Path of Service.* New York: Bell Tower, 1992.

Dass, Ram, and Paul Gorman. *How Can I Help? Stories and Reflections on Service.* New York: Alfred A. Knopf, 1988.

Eisler, Riane. *The Chalice and the Blade: Our History, Our Future.* San Francisco: HarperSanFrancisco, 1988.

Feldman, Christina, and Jack Kornfield, ed. *Stories of the Spirit, Stories of the Heart.* San Francisco: HarperSanFrancisco, 1991.

Fromm, Eric. *The Art of Loving.* New York: Harper and Row, 1956.

Hendrix, Harville. *Getting the Love You Want.* New York: Harper and Row, 1988.

Keen, Sam. *The Passionate Life: The Stages of Loving.* San Francisco: HarperSanFrancisco, 1983.

Scarf, Maggie. *Intimate Partners.* New York: Random House, 1987.

Swimme, Brian. *The Universe Is a Green Dragon.* Sante Fe: Bear and Co., 1984.

Tannen, Deborah. *You Just Don't Understand: Men and Women in Conversation.* New York: William Morrow, 1990.

Wagner, Jane. *The Search for Intelligent Life in the Universe.* New York: Harper and Row, 1986.

Welwood, John, ed. *Challenge of the Heart: Love, Sex, and Intimacy in Changing Times.* Boston: Shambahala, 1985.

Wilbur, Ken. *Grace and Grit.* Boston: Shambahala, 1991.

Suggested Listening

Sounds True Catalog of Audio Tapes. Great Minds on Cassette, 1825 Pearl Street, Boulder, CO 60302.

Other books from CompCare Publishers

•**The Hug Therapy Book** Before Love Therapy there was Hug Therapy: this was the first in the best-selling Hug Therapy series from Kathleen Keating and Mimi Noland. ISBN: 0-89638-065-3, $5.95.

•**Hug Therapy 2** From public demand arose this marvelous sequel in the Hug Therapy series. ISBN: 0-89638-130-7, $5.95

•**The Hug Therapy Book of Birthdays and Anniversaries** The series continues with a delightful gift book for recording special days. ISBN: 0-89638-229-X, $12.95.

•**What's So Funny about Getting Old?** *by Ed Fischer and Jane Thomas Noland* (Mimi's mom!) The best-selling book of cartoons and quips. ISBN: 0-89638-243-5, $6.95

•**Welcome to Club Mom** *by Leslie Lehr Spirson, drawings by Jack Lindstrom.* A humorous and practical guide to pregnancy and the first year of motherhood. ISBN: 0-89638-255-9, $9.95

CompCare Publishers
Call toll free 1-800-328-3330